NewtWit!

Also Compiled by
Tom Connor & Associates

Is Martha Stuart Living?

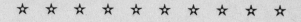

Newt Wit!

Compiled by Tom Connor & Associates

DOUBLEDAY

New York   London   Toronto
Sydney   Auckland

A MAIN STREET BOOK

PUBLISHED BY DOUBLEDAY
a division of
Bantam Doubleday Dell Publishing Group, Inc.
1540 Broadway, New York, New York 10036

MAIN STREET BOOKS, DOUBLEDAY,
and the portrayal of a building with a tree are
trademarks of Doubleday, a division of Bantam
Doubleday Dell Publishing Group, Inc.

Library of Congress Cataloging-in-publication Data
applied for

ISBN 0-385-48005-9

First Main Street Books Edition: February 1995

1 3 5 7 9 10 8 6 4 2

★ ★ ★ ★ ★ ★ ★ ★ ★ ★ ★

NewtWit!

★ ★ ★ ★ ★ ★ ★ ★ ★ ★ ★

Acknowledgments

Thanks to Lisa Grenadier, David Gernert,
Gerald L. Manning, Rick Wolff, Darryl
Manning, Mary Moffitt, Anne Moffitt,
Maureen Kindilien at the Fairfield University
Library, Judith Mandelbaum at Burrelle's
Business Research Center, Joy Haenlein,
John O'Hern, Emily Gordon,
JoAnn Bilyard, and Jim Downey.

★ ★ ★ ★ ★ ★ ★ ★ ★ ★

What Others Say About Newt Gingrich

"Newt Gingrich is the Tonya Harding of politics. If he disapproves of you, he will try to break your knees.
— *New York Post* columnist Jack Newfield (December 9, 1994)

"[Gingrich is] a strategic thinker of the first rank."
— William A. Rusher, Publisher, *National Review*

"There is the Newt Gingrich who is the intellectual, appealing and fun to be with. And there's the Newt Gingrich who is the bloodthirsty partisan who'd just as soon cut your guts out as look at you. And who, very candidly, is mean, mean as hell."
— Lee Howell, former Gingrich press secretary

☆ ☆ ☆ ☆ ☆ ☆ ☆ ☆ ☆ ☆

"A practical man of ideas, a deeply committed conservative with a bold vision of the future, a finely honed ability to communicate and an unusual grasp of political strategy"
— Steven K. Beckner, *Conservative Digest*

"My views of him are somewhat similar to those of a fire hydrant toward a dog."
—Ex-Speaker Jim Wright when asked his feelings about the future Speaker of the House (*Congressional Quarterly Almanac*, 1988)

"The polls say an overwhelming number of Americans do not know who Newt Gingrich is yet. The safest bet in American politics: they will."
(Joe Klein in *Newsweek* December 26, 1994–January 2, 1995)

☆ ☆ ☆ ☆ ☆ ☆ ☆ ☆ ☆ ☆

Affirmative Action

I believe you ought to have affirmative
action on the individual basis based on
economics and culture, not based on race.
I think if you have a poor person from
West Virginia who happens to be white or
a poor person from Harlem who happens
to be black, and they are deserving of a
chance, you ought to bend over
backwards to give them a chance because
from their background, economically and
culturally, they are striving to rise. But to
say, as a matter of pure race, that a
millionaire son or daughter who's black
deserves more preference than a poor
white or a poor Asian or a poor Hispanic
strikes me as madness.

(NBC's *Meet the Press*,December 1, 1991)

☆ ☆ ☆ ☆ ☆ ☆ ☆ ☆ ☆ ☆

American Civilization

People like me are what stand between us and Auschwitz. I see evil around me every day.

(*Atlanta Journal and Constitution*, January 1994)

It is impossible to maintain a civilization with twelve-year-olds having babies, fifteen-year-olds killing each other, seventeen-year-olds dying of AIDS and eighteen-year-olds getting diplomas they can't read.

(*The New York Times*, October 27, 1994)

We are at the edge of losing this civilization. You get two more generations of what we had for the last twenty years and we're in desperate trouble. As long as I believe that's true, I'll keep trying to recruit another generation and train another generation so that when I'm too tired to keep doing this, they'll be ready to step in.

(*Atlanta Journal and Constitution*, January 1994)

The American Dream

My dad's a retired career soldier and we have no great family wealth. And certainly a name like Newt Gingrich is weird enough that it sort of fits the classic American pattern. Maybe there's a long tradition in America with people with unusual backgrounds having an opportunity to rise. But remember, it's not Gingrich alone.

(*CBS This Morning*, November 9, 1994)

☆　☆　☆　☆　☆　☆　☆　☆　☆　☆

[It is] a major, major mistake we've made since World War II to suggest that life is easy and the difficulties are the aberration. I think the opposite is true. I think life is normally hard, and it's the good moments that are the aberration. And that you work hard and you try to raise a family and you try to earn a living and you try to have a safe neighborhood precisely for the good moments. But that a healthy society starts out saying: Life is hard.

(From a motivational tape by Gingrich entitled "History and Leadership"/Quoted in *The Washington Post*, December 19, 1994)

☆ ☆ ☆ ☆ ☆ ☆ ☆ ☆ ☆ ☆

Anti-Poverty Programs

They are a disaster. They ruin the poor.
They create a culture of poverty and a
culture of violence, which is destructive of
this civilization, and they have to be
thoroughly replaced from the ground up.
We need to simply reach out, erase the
slate and start over.

(Commenting on the programs begun in the 1960s
Great Society/*The Washington Post*,
November 12, 1994)

We can reach twice as many kids as
President Clinton is proposing in the
summer jobs program if we enlist the
private sector, and instead of having a
politician's and bureaucrat's jobs program,
we find a way to give a $700 tax credit to
every business that hires a teenager who is
below, say, the school lunch program line.
You could literally double the number of
jobs with no new bureaucracy and no
government effort, but the politicians
wouldn't get the credit for it.

(NBC's *Meet the Press*, February 21, 1993)

The Arts

I think that people who argue that on the one hand you can't allow prayer in school because that'll be subsidizing religion, but on the other hand you have an absolute obligation to subsidize an artist who, as part of his art, urinates on a picture of Christ—those are values most Americans don't understand, period.

(NBC's *Meet the Press*, June 17, 1990)

I think this is an example of some liberals hyperventilating without adequate information. The fact was, it was George Bush's birthday. The press had come in wearing birthday hats, and everybody was having a good time talking about George Bush's birthday making fun of the President on his birthday, and Bob Dole had brought a flag with him. But in fact, it was a birthday event; it was not a flag event.

(Commenting on Senator Bob Kerrey's criticism of a flag-waving incident in the Cabinet Room/ NBC's *Meet the Press*, June 17, 1990)

I personally would privatize them.
> (Response to a question on the future of
> the Corporation for Public Broadcasting and the
> National Endowment for the Arts/ABC's *This Week
> with David Brinkley*, November 13, 1994)

All I'm suggesting is if you want the arts
to survive with federal funding, you
have to assure the average taxpayer that
they are not going to have blasphemy
and egregious obscenity forced down
their throat that they're going to have to
pay for.
> (NBC's *Meet the Press*, June 17, 1990)

I think that the President is correctly
moving to the right position on the
National Endowment for the Arts, that
there is a distinction between subsidy and
censorship.
> (NBC's *Meet the Press*, June 17, 1990)

☆ ☆ ☆ ☆ ☆ ☆ ☆ ☆ ☆ ☆

Baby Boomers

I believe the baby boomers are sick and
tired of being told by liberal politicians
that the only answer's to run up a bigger
deficit for their children and
grandchildren to pay off. And I think
they're ready to say, "Give this generation
a real challenge."

(*CBS This Morning*, September 30, 1994)

I would argue that you can make a very
effective traditional values pitch that child
pornography is obscene, and that those
people ought to be thrown in jail. Most of
my baby-boom friends, when they were
eighteen, would have argued intellectually
at the coffee house that people ought to
be allowed to do what they want to. Now
that they're thirty-seven and they have six-
year-olds, they're real tough on child
pornography. I can carry the baby
boomers. I could kill Gary Hart in that
group, on those issues.

(*Mother Jones*, November 1984)

☆　☆　☆　☆　☆　☆　☆　☆　☆　☆

Bipartisanism

We want to work with the President of the
United States. You only get one President
at a time, and we ought to be able to take
one year off, it seems to me, from
presidential politics and spend 1995
actually trying to pass things, working
together for America.

> (NBC's *Campaign '94*: Election Night,
> November 8, 1994)

We ought to be able to find some
bipartisan ways early on to build a sense
of confidence that the American system
does work, that the American voters have
an impact, but that all of us have an
obligation in 1995 to work together for
the American voters, and to let the '96
presidential campaign come in '96.

> (NBC's *Today*, November 9, 1994)

☆ ☆ ☆ ☆ ☆ ☆ ☆ ☆ ☆ ☆

Blacks

For too long it has been possible for American schoolchildren who happen to be black [to walk through the Capitol] and not see anyone in this Capitol stand for them.

(Commenting on a House vote to place a bust or statue of civil rights leader the Reverend Dr. Martin Luther King, Jr., in the Capitol/Quoted in the 1981 *Congressional Quarterly*)

One of them said to me—and I think every white American needs to understand this: He goes home. He goes into, say, a first-, second-, third-grade class. Every fourth young black boy in that class is going to end up dead or in jail unless something changes. I mean, he looks around this room with little kids, seven, eight, nine years old, innocent, and the statistics are so tragic, whether it's Atlanta or Baltimore or New York or Chicago or Los Angeles—and not just blacks, but Hispanics and, to some extent, poor whites. And you look at that and you say we—and right here in D.C.—we've got to do something.

(ABC's *Nightline*, November 29, 1994)

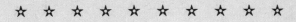

Bosnia

Peace through strength has to start with local strength and the local people's ability to defend themselves. I think that makes a lot of sense if we're both arming and training the Bosnian Muslims so that they're capable of surviving.

(CBS's *Face the Nation*, May 9, 1993)

And I'm still against going into Bosnia. Bosnia is a total mess. Bosnian Muslims shoot Croats and Serbs. Serbs shoot Croats and Bosnian Muslims. You've got all three sides killing each other.

(ABC's *Nightline*, July 12, 1993)

I think the role of a superpower is to act decisively with overwhelming force to win the engagement with minimum casualties to our own men and women while inflicting on the enemy a decisive and unalterable defeat. There are a lot of things we can't affect in the world. I think Bosnia is one of them.

(ABC's *Nightline*, July 12, 1993)

☆ ☆ ☆ ☆ ☆ ☆ ☆ ☆ ☆ ☆

Budget

I don't think that this government at this
time has the moral authority to ask
families to squeeze their family budget
because the government refuses to
squeeze its own budget.

(NBC's *Meet the Press*, February 21, 1993)

Now, everybody in this country knows
their family budget doesn't automatically
grow. If you go to a straight line
budgeting, if you simply set up a system
where you require that every new dollar
other than Social Security—that every new
dollar be considered an addition, I think
you can exercise fiscal discipline.

(NBC's *Meet the Press*, October 2, 1994)

I would rather shrink the federal
government and give a cost-of-living
increase to the people we want to keep than
punish every federal worker—the AIDS
researcher, the cancer researcher, the border
patrolman, the air traffic controller—
because we can't figure out a way to
downside the bureaucracies in the cities.

(NBC's *Meet the Press*, February 21, 1993)

The 1992 elections sent a signal that the American people want change, and it sent a signal that the American people want to get towards a balanced budget, they want to control the deficit, they want to start being responsible for what we're spending, and that if you're for change, one of the major changes [is that] this city has to be setting priorities and paying for what you're doing, and that's a very big dividing line between the past and future.

(CBS's *Face the Nation*, July 25, 1993)

☆ ☆ ☆ ☆ ☆ ☆ ☆ ☆ ☆ ☆

Bureaucracy

You can have an active, aggressive,
conservative state which does not in fact
have a large centralized bureaucracy ...
This goes back to Teddy Roosevelt. We
have not seen an activist conservative
presidency since TR.

> (*Mother Jones*, November 1984)

I believe that local communities should
have the opportunity to apply local
common sense without a Washington
bureaucracy.

> (ABC's *This Week with David Brinkley*,
> November 13, 1994)

I think it's inevitable that the bureaucracy,
which really is a welfare state bureaucracy,
will resist, fight, kick, scream in terms of
trying to get the right kind of legislation.

> ("CBS This Morning", February 27, 1992)

I'm wearing a Habitat for Humanity
button. They're volunteers doing
something real without the federal
government, and I'm just suggesting to

you that there are a lot of answers in this country that aren't federal bureaucracies putting out federal regulations in Washington, D.C.

(ABC's Nightline, November 29, 1994)

The current system has failed. Children in Washington, D.C., will go tomorrow morning to schools that fail; they will live in neighborhoods that are violent; they'll have a future that is desperate, and we ought to break out of it. And I'm prepared to reach out and cooperate with anybody who wants to break out of it. What I won't do is spend more money on a federal bureaucracy to have a Washington-based solution that we already know before it starts is a failure.

(ABC's Nightline, November 29, 1994)

☆ ☆ ☆ ☆ ☆ ☆ ☆ ☆ ☆ ☆ ☆

George Bush

He is the best all-around politician I've ever seen.

> (NBC's *Meet the Press*, December 1, 1991)

If I were betting, I would bet that by late next summer, George Bush will be a very formidable candidate, and I would bet a lot that he will be elected President.

> (NBC's *Meet the Press*, December 1, 1991)

The reason we're in a mess is when the country continues to send to the White House Presidents who are committed to a center-right coalition, they continue to send to the Capitol a union-left coalition of Democrats who are antithetical; we're just deadlocked. We get nothing done.

> (Commenting on President Bush/NBC's *Meet the Press*, December 1, 1991)

"Martel smiled as he thought about him. He hadn't been the cleverest flight leader in the fleet, but by God he knew how to lead a group straight into enemy flank like

☆ ☆ ☆ ☆ ☆ ☆ ☆ ☆ ☆ ☆

they were on rails. What was his name? …
Lieutenant George Bush. Quite a guy, in
his goofy way."
(From a draft of a World War II novel cowritten by
Gingrich/Quoted in *The Washington Post*,
December 2, 1994)

Jimmy Carter

Without a doubt, the most consistent
citizen of our former Presidents. If you
watch him, you get a little shamed into
being a better citizen yourself.
(To his Saturday morning class at Kennesaw State
College/*Atlanta Journal and Constitution*,
November 28, 1993)

Change

We will not make it through your lifetime
without radical change. You're either
going to force the changes or your
generation is going to suffer a long, steady
decline in the quality of life.
(Comments made to the Capitol Hill Club, 1992)

☆ ☆ ☆ ☆ ☆ ☆ ☆ ☆ ☆ ☆

Civil Rights Act

I think that this is a country which is about 85 percent antiquota, and for the life of me, I do not understand why the liberal Democrats cling to that. I think that they ought to help us pass a clean civil rights bill that everyone can agree has no quotas in it. That's the significant change in public policy, back towards an integrated America in which every individual has an opportunity, but without regard to any kind of racial background.

(ABC's *This Week with David Brinkley*,
March 10, 1991)

☆ ☆ ☆ ☆ ☆ ☆ ☆ ☆ ☆ ☆

Clinton Administration

This administration is strategically in the position of Richard Nixon in 1969. There was a three-way race for President. This candidate got 43 percent. He does not represent a majority, he does not represent the popular will.

> (NBC's *Meet the Press*, February 21, 1993)

I just want to make the point that this administration sort of talks loudly and carries a smaller stick.

> (Commenting on the Clinton administrations's foreign policy/*CBS This Morning*, May 4, 1994)

It's a sad comment on the Clinton administration that they had an enormous opportunity to bring about change and they failed. And I don't say that harshly.

> (*The Washington Post*, November 10, 1994)

I've been, frankly, shocked by the administration's inability to decide what its priorities are. At one point, remember, it had a fight with China about human rights, a fight with Japan about trade, and a fight with North Korea about nuclear weapons. Now you can't pick fights with all three countries simultaneously. You've got to have some priority.

(CBS's *Face the Nation*, May 29, 1994)

I don't know how good this team would be if they had a President who was willing to be part of a team, but my sense is that you have Saturday morning sessions where they sit around and drink coffee, they make up some press release, send it out and then tell the Pentagon or the State Department about the policy they've invented. Now, if you have a President who's not willing to be a disciplined, systematic part of a team, I don't care how good his subordinates are, they're going to be faced with chaos every week.

(CBS's *Face the Nation*, May 29, 1994)

☆　☆　☆　☆　☆　☆　☆　☆　☆　☆

President Bill Clinton

He listens as well as any President I've
ever seen.
> (Commenting on a meeting with Bill Clinton/
> *The New Yorker*, September 5, 1994)

There's a part of him that's just
automatically compassionate with anybody.
It's transactional, it has no policy meaning.
> (*The New Yorker*, September 5, 1994)

You have to love people enough to want
to change them, not just feel their pain.
> (Comments made directly about the film *Boys' Town*
> on the TNT network, and indirectly about
> President Clinton/*Time*, January 9, 1995)

Well, I'm a college teacher. I think I'd
probably give him a C+
> (Grading Clinton/NBC's *Sunday Today*,
> January 23, 1994)

☆ ☆ ☆ ☆ ☆ ☆ ☆ ☆ ☆ ☆

There is no evidence, whether it's gays in the military or taxing senior citizens on Social Security, there is no evidence that Bill Clinton ever made clear to this country what his agenda was until after he got elected.

(NBC's *Meet the Press*, February 21, 1993)

He has no claim to suggest he has a popular mandate.

(NBC's *Meet the Press*, February 21, 1993)

The President of the United States has to have a constancy of purpose and a clarity of language, because the nation has to know what to expect... I desperately hope he will calm down and settle down, decide what he's going to do and stick to it and use honest language to honestly communicate with all Americans. It's going to be better for the country.

(NBC's *Meet the Press*, February 21, 1993)

☆　☆　☆　☆　☆　☆　☆　☆　☆　☆

First of all, he is a great politician, and you can't deny that Bill Clinton has terrific personal skills in the business of politics. Second, we have an economy which has been recovering. You can argue it's the Bush recovery, but nonetheless, it's recovering, and he's President during the recovery, and we're not at war.

(NBC's *Sunday Today*, January 23, 1994)

What you got was Dukakis with a Southern accent.

(*The New York Times*, July 24, 1994)

When I hear a Clinton speech, I'm normally applauding and saying, "Boy, I agree with that."

(ABC's *This Week with David Brinkley*, January 2, 1995)

McGoverniks.

(On the Clinton's/Quoted by the *Boston Sunday Globe*, January 1, 1995)

★ ★ ★ ★ ★ ★ ★ ★ ★ ★

Since the election I've used the term McGovernite, not McGovernik. It was one of those things that the *Times* picked up and therefore it's now history. I didn't say that to attack the President.

(ABC's Nightline, November 29, 1994)

Hillary Rodham Clinton

She [Connie Chung] says to my mother, who spent eight hours with her—my dad baked her a cake—she says, "Whisper it to me." My mother's not a professional politician, she's not a national figure, she's not a millionaire television correspondent. My mother's just a simple woman who loves her son ... I think CBS shouldn't run that. I think it is unprofessional and disreputable.

(On CBS correspondent Connie Chung
eliciting from Gingrich's mother the fact that he
referred to Hillary Clinton as "a bitch"/
CBS This Morning, January 4, 1995)

My advice [to her] would be simply to look at Eleanor Roosevelt, look at people who've been very effective as first lady, and then carve out a very specific area that she wants to really work on and do so in an open, bipartisan way. And I think if they'll learn these lessons that she could have a very successful two or six years, depending on whether or not they get reelected.

(*CBS Evening News*, November 28, 1994)

I think it's perfectly appropriate for the President to ask his wife to take a major role. I'd rather have her influence out in the open rather than have it hidden away in the back room.

(*Atlanta Journal and Constitution*, May 5, 1993)

☆ ☆ ☆ ☆ ☆ ☆ ☆ ☆ ☆ ☆

Congress

We're a little like Sears Roebuck or any
other consumer-oriented company. We
have a wide range of people who want our
help, and we have a steady increase in
customer service.

(PBS's *Congress: We the People*, 1989)

The fact is that all over the world, whether
it's Italy or it's Japan or it's the United
States, people are sick of corruption in
politics. There's a much higher standard
being promulgated. It's hard, I think, for
all of us to learn to live with these new
standards, but every time there is another
scandal, every time there is another
conviction or indictment, the public's
belief in the Congress is diminished a little
more. I think people are increasingly fed
up with the Congress.

(ABC's *Nightline*, July 26, 1993)

☆ ☆ ☆ ☆ ☆ ☆ ☆ ☆ ☆ ☆

104th Congress

We'll know in six months or a year
whether we are able to perform in the way
that the American people really respond
to. We could have a great day and fall on
our face later on, we could have a day of
real learning and do brilliantly later on.

(NBC's *Today*, January 4,. 1995)

Contract with America

We're actually going to keep our word.

(*USA Today*, January 5, 1995)

☆ ☆ ☆ ☆ ☆ ☆ ☆ ☆ ☆ ☆

Crime

The President should announce we're going to build stockades and military bases using military construction, and that by June 1 of this year, no state and no locality should release a single violent criminal prior to the end of their sentence because of lack of space. We can charge per diem to the states. Let's get this done. We own the land. We have the equipment. We have the troops. Let's build stockades. They don't have to have television. They don't have to have air-conditioning. These are holding pens for violent people for whom we don't have the space.

(NBC's *Sunday Today*, January 23, 1994)

We were thinking, This is good. You know, this is like watching the President get into his Mustang and drive straight into a ditch. You say, "Oh, look at that!"

(On observing the temporary derailment of President Clinton's crime bill with fellow Republicans/*The New Yorker*, September 5, 1994)

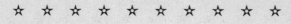

Critics

I understand my critics are fixated and
pathologically disoriented, but they are my
opponents. Why would I try to correct that?
(Time, October 10, 1994)

Democrats

Democrats are the enemy of normal
Americans. A better quote might have
been to have said middle-class Americans,
but there's no question that the Clinton
administration—I was talking specifically
about the Clinton administration—is seen
by most middle-class Americans as
antithetical to their values, their
pocketbook and their future.
(CBS's *Face the Nation*, October 23, 1994)

I just want to be blunt. I mean, this is a
Democratic machine political scandal.
Both in the House bank, which was a
patronage operation, and in the House
post office.
(ABC's *This Week with David Brinkley*,
March 15, 1992)

The House Democrats are obsessed with me. It's almost funny how much they fear me.

(*Time*, October 10, 1994)

They don't share any information, they don't share any responsibility, they don't share any power.

(ABC's *This Week with David Brinkley*, March 15, 1992)

If, in fact, we are to follow the Chamberlain liberal Democratic line of withdrawal from the planet, we would truly have tyranny everywhere and we in America could experience the joys of Soviet-style brutality and murdering of women and children.

(*Congressional Record*, October 27, 1983)

★ ★ ★ ★ ★ ★ ★ ★ ★ ★

The fact is the Democratic party has controlled the U.S. House since I was eleven years old. I'm now forty-seven. Since 1954, their Speaker has set the schedule, decided what comes to the floor, decided who chaired the committees. And the Democrats have the ability, next week if they want to, to bring forth a crime and drug package. I think "Congress" is all too often a euphemism for Democratic Party leadership on Capitol Hill.

(NBC's *Today*, June 21, 1990)

The fact is that a liberal Democrat doesn't want to talk about ideology because they don't want to explain publicly what they're really doing.

(NBC's *Meet the Press*, December 1, 1991)

I believe that the institutional control of the House by the current Democratic leadership makes it impossible to reform the House and people need to confront that.

(ABC's *This Week with David Brinkley*, March 15, 1992)

The Democratic leadership only shares information after it appears in print.
> (ABC's *This Week with David Brinkley*,
> March 15, 1992)

This is a nineteenth-century institution which has been protected and hidden from the public, and each successive onion layer that's peeled off, the country gets madder at the Congress. It sooner or later has to have a reform administration that cleans the whole place up.
> (ABC's *This Week with David Brinkley*,
> March 15, 1992)

I am saying to you that there is an institutional problem of corruption of power involving the Democratic leadership. It's caused them to have a Speaker and a Whip resign in the last Congress. It is still there. It leads to cover-ups. It leads to a kind of behavior which is unacceptable to the American people, and if a reform Democrat's serious, they need to vote for Bob Michel to have a reform speakership.
> (ABC's *This Week with David Brinkley*,
> March 15, 1992)

★ ★ ★ ★ ★ ★ ★ ★ ★ ★

The guys who are failing you on every front can't manage the capitol. So they have managed to both screw up the capitol and screw up your lives, and it's their fault.

(Congressional candidates' training session, April 1992)

We don't particularly want to have a single ounce of compromise with those who still believe that they can somehow improve and prop up and make work a bureaucratic welfare state, and a counterculture set of values which are literally killing the poor.

(ABC's *Nightline*, November 29, 1994)

On the one hand, there is a Republican Party that believes in opportunities and possibilities. On the other hand, there is a Democratic Party that rejects the lessons of American history, despises the values of the American people and denies the basic goodness of the American nation.

(ABC's *Nightline*, November 29, 1994)

☆ ☆ ☆ ☆ ☆ ☆ ☆ ☆ ☆ ☆

We were faced with a system that was corrupt. The system refused to respond to the country as it changed. We adopted a series of positions that were very popular in the country—a balanced-budget amendment, a line-item veto, no tax increases—and the corrupt Democratic machine that should have responded remained rigid and stuck in place. It then won an accidental election for President with 43 percent of the vote, and instead of moving to the center, which would have required analyzing the Perot vote, which was antigovernment and for cutting spending, it moved to the left.

(*The New York Times*, July 24, 1994)

★ ★ ★ ★ ★ ★ ★ ★ ★ ★

The greatest leaders in fighting for an integrated America in the twentieth century were in the Democratic Party. The fact is, it was the liberal wing of the Democratic Party that ended segregation. The fact is that it was Franklin Delano Roosevelt who gave hope to a nation that was in despair and could have slid into dictatorship. And the fact is, every Republican has much to learn from studying what the Democrats did right.

(Excerpt from Gingrich's speech on the opening day of the 104th Congress, *The New York Times*, January 5, 1995)

These people are sick. They are destructive of the values we believe in. They are so consumed by their own power, by a Mussolini-like ego, that their willingness to run over normal human beings and to destroy honest institutions is unending.

(*Rolling Stone*, June 15, 1989)

☆ ☆ ☆ ☆ ☆ ☆ ☆ ☆ ☆ ☆

Robert Dole

[He's] the tax collector for the welfare
state.

(*The Washington Post*, January 3, 1985)

Bob Dole [is] unequivocally the hardest-
working and, I think, an extraordinarily
effective Republican leader.

(ABC's *This Week with David Brinkley*,
November 13, 1994)

No, but I'm very much ready to serve [as]
Speaker for his presidency. We both care
deeply about the Republican Party, we
care deeply about returning power to the
American people, and we've both proven
it by committing years of our life. You're
going to see us work very hard to work
together. I don't think we need to rush
into the '96 presidential race and I'm
willing to say, up front, Senator Dole's
going to be a candidate.

(Responding when asked if he will endorse or
back up Dole if Dole decides to run for President/
CBS This Morning, January 4, 1995)

Drug Use

That was a sign we were alive and were in graduate school in that era.

> (On his admission that he had smoked marijuana/
> NBC's *Meet the Press*, December 4, 1994)

My point is, you've got scattered throughout this administration counterculture people. I had a senior law enforcement official tell me that, in his judgment, up to a quarter of the White House staff, when they first came in, had used drugs in the last four or five years.

> (NBC's *Meet the Press*/December 4, 1994)

David Duke

David Duke is a Nazi Klansman who ... is despicable and should be shunned in American politics.

> (NBC's *Meet the Press*, December 1, 1991)

☆ ☆ ☆ ☆ ☆ ☆ ☆ ☆ ☆ ☆

Economics

Is supply-side economics finished? Only
in the sense that General George S.
Patton's army was finished in Germany in
May 1945.

> (Quoted in *The 1989 Conservative Calendar*)

Eisenhower

My uncle taught me to smile at
Eisenhower on the television and to turn
Adlai Stevenson off.

> (*The Washington Post*, December 18, 1994)

I'd like to have Eisenhower's humanness.
One of the reasons I keep reading
Eisenhower is that he was very successful
at getting along with people who despised
him.

> (*The Washington Post*, January 3, 1985)

Ethics

It's a devastating issue if you're on the wrong side of it.

(Washington Today: "The Complications of Being Newt," December 2, 1994)*

I don't think I'm a Savonarola. I don't think I have any great interest in running around and finding sin.

(The New York Times, August 23, 1992)*

It is perfectly American to be wrong.

(Mother Jones, November 1984)*

[A] pathetically narrow partisan gimmick.

(Response to the outcry over his $4.5 million book deal/USA Today, January 5, 1995)*

If the only people allowed to write news stories were those who had never told a lie, we wouldn't have many stories. If the only people allowed to serve on juries were saints, we wouldn't have any juries.

(Mother Jones, November 1984)*

★ ★ ★ ★ ★ ★ ★ ★ ★ ★

If I announce today I was buying vanilla ice cream for every child in America, David Bonior would jump up and say he wants them all to have heart attacks some-day.

(On Democrats' criticism of his $4.5 million book deal with HarperCollins/*The Washington Post*, December 31, 1994)

I'm not going to be a masochist and say, "Please give me the lowest possible rate," so that *The New York Times* editorial board thinks I'm OK.

(On decision to return most of $4.5 million advance from the book deal but earn a higher royalty/ *The New York Times*, December 30, 1994)

Being tried in public is wrong.

(ABC's *Nightline*, July 26, 1993)

☆ ☆ ☆ ☆ ☆ ☆ ☆ ☆ ☆ ☆

Family Values

I'm going to marry her.

(Told to friend Jim Tilton on seeing his high school
geometry teacher and future wife, Jackie Battley, on
the first day of class/*The Washington Post*,
December 18, 1994)

She's not young enough or pretty enough
to be the wife of a President. And besides,
she has cancer.

(Comment on divorcing his first wife
widely reported to have been made to
former aide Kip Carter. Gingrich
denies having made the statement.)

I mean, one of the things we know
historically, biologically, is that males are
designed to be relatively irresponsible and
every healthy society on the planet tries to
maximize male responsibility.

(NPR's *Morning Edition*, August 28, 1992)

Family values and extended families are a
major key to success and to the stability
and to ending crime and—and having
healthy economic growth.

(NPR's *Morning Edition*, August 28, 1992)

☆ ☆ ☆ ☆ ☆ ☆ ☆ ☆ ☆ ☆

My closest and strongest personal adviser
is my wife.

> (NBC's *Meet the Press*, October 3, 1993)

The Flag

Most Americans would argue that the flag
communicates an emotional value worthy
of sustaining and protecting.

> (NBC's *Meet the Press*, June 17, 1990)

Gays in the Republican Party

I'd welcome any citizen. I'm against any
law which gives you a legal status based
on your sexual behavior.

> (NBC's *Meet the Press*, December 4, 1994)

☆ ☆ ☆ ☆ ☆ ☆ ☆ ☆ ☆ ☆

Newt Gingrich

If you decide in your freshman year in
high school that your job is to spend your
lifetime trying to change the future of your
people, you're probably fairly weird. I
think I was pretty weird as a kid.
>   (*The Washington Post*, January 3, 1985)

I saw *Sands of Iwo Jima* four times in one
day. And I think I identified that version
of [John] Wayne with my stepfather, as a
totally heroic person who was aloof and
distant but doing something very
important.]
>   (In response to his stepfather's comment that
>   as a boy Gingrich always tried to walk like
>   John Wayne/*The Washington Post*,
>   December 18, 1994)

I am a moderate.
>   (To Atlanta reporters on election night, 1978/
>   *The Washington Post*, December 19, 1994)

[I'm an] American Gaullist.
>   (*Newsweek*, January 9, 1995)

51

☆　☆　☆　☆　☆　☆　☆　☆　☆　☆

I see myself as representing the conservative
wing of the post-industrial society.
(*Mother Jones*, November 1984)

I am essentially a revolutionary.
(*The New York Times*, August 23, 1992)

I will be somewhat less confrontational,
and somewhat less abrasive in the future,
because I am no longer the person I once
was, and it will take two to five years for
my reputation to catch up, and in some
ways it never will.
(Speaking about becoming the "new" Newt/
The Washington Post, January 1, 1985)

How would you use who I am becoming?
(Comments made to advisers following a speech to a
group of admirers/*Time*, January 9, 1995)

I've been seen as a partisan and I am a
partisan, obviously, because, a) I've been
trapped in the House, which is a very
partisan environment, for my entire public
career in Washington, and, b) because
under Reagan and Bush, it was their job to
do the vision and it was my job to be a
partisan soldier. That era is over.
(*The New York Times*, October 27, 1994)

52

☆ ☆ ☆ ☆ ☆ ☆ ☆ ☆ ☆ ☆

I think I am a transformational figure. I think I am trying to effect a change so large that the people who would be hurt by the change, the liberal machine, have a natural reaction.

(October 17 interview/*The Washington Post*, December 20, 1994)

I'm a modernizer who is suggesting that we leap back an entire span and claim our own heritage again...I believe in institutions. I believe in the Republican Party and the House of Representatives, and I think that strengthening the one will strengthen the other. If all I were going to do is bail out the ship while it keeps sinking, I would just as soon quit and get on the life raft.

(Quoted in *Changing of the Guard: Power and Leadership in America* by David S. Broder, Simon & Schuster, 1980))

☆ ☆ ☆ ☆ ☆ ☆ ☆ ☆ ☆ ☆

It was the most amazing decision of my life. And it gives me certain inner strengths that other politicians don't have, because I see this as a calling, as something that someone has to do if America is to keep the freedoms we believe in.

(On his call to politics, at age fifteen, upon visiting the World War I site of Verdun, France/ *Mother Jones*, November 1984)

I think there's an almost fervent effort by some media institutions to prove that in some way I'm a hypocrite. I'm not a saint. I mean, I'm a pretty normal person.

(*CBS Evening News*, November 29, 1994)

I have an enormous personal ambition. I want to shift the entire planet. And I'm doing it. I am now a famous person ... I represent real power.

(January 1985/Quoted in The *Washington Post*, December 20, 1994)

I'm a hawk, but I'd like to be a smart cheap hawk. I don't particularly want to be a dumb wasteful hawk.

(NBC's *Meet the Press*, February 21, 1993)

I love talks that are probably too long for politics, I like ideas, I think books are important, I'm willing to occasionally pay the price of being controversial in order to get people thinking and get things moving.

(NBC's Today, January 4, 1995)

God and Religion

I would say to you unequivocally—it will probably sound pious and sanctimonious saying it—I am a sinner. I am a normal person. I am like everyone else I ever met. One of the reasons I go to God is that I ain't very good—I'm not perfect.

(Mother Jones, November 1984)

I'm not a very strong believer.

(Commenting on his direction to a speech-
writer to remove all references to God/
Mother Jones, November 1984)

Our liberal national elite doesn't believe in religion.

(Quoted in Mother Jones, November 1984, from a
U.S. News and World Report interview)

★　★　★　★　★　★　★　★　★　★

There is a matter of principle that says you should not raise tax money from a citizen to force them to pay for blasphemy, for example, which I find much more offensive than obscenity.

(NBC's *Meet the Press*, June 17, 1990)

I do have a vision of an America in which a belief in the Creator is once again at the center of defining being an American.

(*The Village Voice*, January 10, 1995)

☆ ☆ ☆ ☆ ☆ ☆ ☆ ☆ ☆ ☆

Government

If we're serious about balancing the budget and we're serious about cutting the size of government, then guess what? We're going to have to change government dramatically.

(NBC's *Meet the Press*, October 2, 1994)

I think that the eighties demonstrated in the Soviet Union and Poland and Czechoslovakia and Hungary that large, centralized government bureaucracies don't create jobs very well, and that pouring money into large big-city political machines is about the worst possible way to create jobs.

(NBC's *Today*, June 3, 1992)

One of our goals is to shrink the congressional staffs enough to sell one of the two House annexes. Now I think the act of selling a government congressional office building sends the right kind of signal.

(NBC's *Meet the Press*,. December 4, 1994)

☆ ☆ ☆ ☆ ☆ ☆ ☆ ☆ ☆ ☆

I think we ought to bring in ten of the people who have been down sizing IBM, Xerox, General Motors; ask them exactly how to apply it, and go for a goal of dramatically fewer federal employees, just as there are dramatically fewer middle-management people at those other places. That would save over five years a dramatic amount of money ... And I'd have the same kind of people who are going to downsize the civilian bureaucracy looking at the Pentagon bureaucracy. I don't think any place ought to be sacred.

(NBC interview with Tom Brokaw on Gingrich's impression of Clinton's economic plan, February 17, 1993)

Gun Control

I won't support gun control because the only people it's going to affect are middle-class, law-abiding citizens. If we lock up all the violent criminals and we have enough prisons built and that doesn't work, then I'm prepared to look at gun control.

(ABC's *This Week with David Brinkley*, January 2, 1994)

Health Care

You cannot get to universal coverage
without a police state.

(ABC's *This Week with David Brinkley*,
August 14, 1994)

Don't let yourselves be the sheep to be
sheared.

(Advice to a gathering of one thousand members of
the American Medical Association, *Journal of the
American Medical Association*, April 21, 1993)

I told 1,200 doctors that the AMA
brought in about three weeks ago, "You
are either going to Wal-Mart or you are
going to go to a Canadian bureaucracy,
but you're not going to stay where you
are."

(*Atlanta Journal and Constitution*, May 5, 1993)

✩　✩　✩　✩　✩　✩　✩　✩　✩　✩

Anita Hill

[Here] you have a person who was
contacted by the Democratic staff, who
made relatively mild allegations in her
initial statement, which she was told
would be kept confidential … In the end,
she could not prove her allegation.

(ABC's *Nightline*, October 15, 1991)

Most women have decided that Anita Hill
was not telling the truth, most men have
decided she was not telling the truth,
blacks have decided by a larger margin
than whites that she's not telling the truth.
Now, I feel very sorry for Professor Hill,
but the fact is, with three solid days of
television coverage, the country got to
listen to the story and it formed its
opinion.

(ABC's *Nightline*, October 15, 1991)

☆ ☆ ☆ ☆ ☆ ☆ ☆ ☆ ☆ ☆

Humanitarianism

We have a humanitarian interest in the seven-year-old in New York who was murdered the other day by a criminal who was put back out on the street by the government. We have a lot of places where we have humanitarian interests, starting with Atlanta, Georgia, and St. Louis, and New York. And we're not doing that great a job being humanitarian for a lot of people in America.

(CBS's *Face the Nation*, May 9. 1993)

Saddam Hussein

I think, in retrospect, we would have been much better off to have forced his departure from the government as a condition of the cease-fire.

(CBS's *Face the Nation*, May 9, 1993)

☆ ☆ ☆ ☆ ☆ ☆ ☆ ☆ ☆ ☆

Inner Cities

It seems to me that there's an awful lot
that the big cities can do to get themselves
in order and to get their own house in
order before they turn to the rest of the
country for more money.

(NBC's *Today*, June 3, 1992)

First of all I think I represent the interest
of everybody in America who cares
passionately about whether it's the poorest
child not getting prenatal care, or the
young man who doesn't have a hope of
getting a job or the suburbanite who runs
a real risk of having their entire world
collapse because, you know, you can't live
in a country like that if you have the kind
of dangers we now have in some of our
biggest cities.

(NBC's *Today*, June 3, 1992)

☆ ☆ ☆ ☆ ☆ ☆ ☆ ☆ ☆ ☆

International Trade

The fact is, there are some countries we have big surpluses with, there are some countries we run deficits with. I want us to kick in the Japanese door to compete more in Japan to create American jobs, but that ought to be a dynamic process, that shouldn't be us saying to their government, "Solve it or we're going to cut out 1,250,000 cars a year," which is what John Dingell would do, tell the American consumers we're going to punish them because the Japanese government doesn't muscle its car companies and because our car companies aren't being as competitive as they ought to.

(ABC's *Nightline*, January 6, 1992)

☆ ☆ ☆ ☆ ☆ ☆ ☆ ☆ ☆ ☆

Rush Limbaugh

My opinion of Rush, expressed publicly
and privately, is that he is a serious man
and a major political force for the
conservative movement who understands
the role of humor and showmanship in
mass communication.

> (Letters to the editor, *Atlanta Journal and
> Constitution*, July 6, 1993)

The Media

The American people are more patient
than the American news media.

> (NBC's *Today*, January 4, 1995)

Medicare

Why should a $20,000-a-year worker with
two children have their taxes transferred
to Frank Sinatra or David Rockefeller to
pay for the Medicare premiums?

> (ABC's *This Week with David Brinkley*,
> January 10, 1993)

☆ ☆ ☆ ☆ ☆ ☆ ☆ ☆ ☆ ☆

The Military

Politicians tell soldiers what the ground rules are.

(*The Washington Post*, December 18, 1994)

Mission

[To] renew American civilization and redirect the fate of the human race.

(*The New York Times*, October 27, 1994)

This is really hard, making this happen—educating, reeducating, over and over, making a mistake, having to reanalyze. I'm trying to educate a nation in the skills of self-government. Starting November 9th, if I'm Speaker, we have to live this. We will have a much bigger burden. People really want to know where we go. Every day we have to be that transformation, not just talk it, and we will make mistakes and I'm very worried about how to do it.

(*The New York Times*, October 27, 1994)

★　★　★　★　★　★　★　★　★　★

The real success is in the morning we wake up on a Monday and no child has been killed anywhere in America that weekend, and every child is going to a school their parents think is worth attending, and across the country there is a smaller, more customer-friendly government doing effectively what government should do, and every American has a chance to create a job or find a job, and across the planet freedom is winning and civility and decency are driving barbarism out of our lives, then we will truly succeed.

(Upon accepting the nomination of Republicans to be Speaker of the House/ *The New York Times*, December 5, 1994

George Mitchell

George Mitchell is to the left of Yeltsin.
(NBC's *Meet the Press*, December 1, 1991)

☆ ☆ ☆ ☆ ☆ ☆ ☆ ☆ ☆ ☆

Morality

We are in deep trouble as a society.
(*Mother Jones*, November 1984)

People are looking for a guidepost as to
how they should live, how their institutions
should behave, and who they should follow.
(*Mother Jones*, November 1984)

How can any American read about an
eleven-year-old buried with his teddy bear
because he killed a fourteen-year-old and
then another fourteen-year-old killed him,
and not have some sense of, my God,
where has this country gone? How can we
not decide that this is a moral crisis equal
to segregation, equal to slavery? And how
can we not insist that every day we take
steps to do something?
(Excerpt from Gingrich's speech on the opening day
of the 104th Congress/*The New York Times*,
January 5, 1995)

☆ ☆ ☆ ☆ ☆ ☆ ☆ ☆ ☆ ☆

National Budget

I think the Democrats couldn't stand the
prospect of spending Friday, Saturday and
Sunday before an election still in session
with the country noticing that, despite
Democratic leadership of both the House
and the Senate, they can't pass a signable
budget.

(NPR's *All Things Considered*, October 11, 1990)

☆ ☆ ☆ ☆ ☆ ☆ ☆ ☆ ☆ ☆

National Deficit

It is impossible to grow your way out of
these deficits as long as the Democrats
control the Congress because they will
spend.

> (ABC's *This Week with David Brinkley*,
> December 22, 1991)

Since they've controlled the House since
1954, it's always been their deficit.
Because the Democrats originate all tax
bills and all spending bills in the House.

> (ABC's *This Week with David Brinkley*,
> January 10, 1993)

The principle of encouraging the creation
of jobs and the principle of having
incentives so that jobs are created in the
private sector is as important as ever. If we
have a very deep recession, I don't care
what budget package we pass, the deficit's
going to increase. So I have yet to see a
single study that suggests that you can
have a deep recession and do anything to
cope with the deficit.

> (NPR's *All Things Considered*, October 11, 1990)

☆ ☆ ☆ ☆ ☆ ☆ ☆ ☆ ☆ ☆

Orphanages

I'd ask her [Hillary Clinton] to rent the
Mickey Rooney movie about Boys' Town.
I don't understand liberals who live in
enclaves of safety who say, "Oh, this
would be a terrible thing. Look at the
Norman Rockwell family that would break
up." And the fact is, we are allowing a
brutalization and a degradation of
children in this country, a destructiveness.
We say to a thirteen-year-old drug addict
who's pregnant, you know, "Put your baby
in the dumpster, that's OK, but we're not
going to give you a boarding school, we're
not going to give you a place for that child
to grow up." There is no place there.
Wouldn't it be better for that girl ... to
have had a place where she could go to
and say, "I'm not prepared to raise a child.
Would you please raise this child?"
instead of dumping it in a dumpster?

(NBC's *Meet the Press*, December 4, 1994)

☆ ☆ ☆ ☆ ☆ ☆ ☆ ☆ ☆ ☆

Bob Packwood

What it is basically saying is, "Don't write anything down. Don't keep anything. And burn anything you might happen to have."

(On congressional move to have Senator Packwood hand over his diary/CBS's *Face the Nation*, October 31, 1993)

Politics

In every election in American history, both parties have their cliches. The party that has the cliches that ring true wins. And if the cliches continue to ring true when the party governs, then that party and those cliches can change history.

(*The New York Times*, July 31 , 1988)

In some ways, this is a lonely, painful business. I canceled all tomorrow's business to go home because I decided I had been away from Marianne too long. She has a real back problem and she's feeling lonely.

(*The Washington Post*, January 3, 1985)

☆　☆　☆　☆　☆　☆　☆　☆　☆　☆

If you live your life as a hostage to everybody else's decision, you either have to live a very narrow life or you have to spend a lot of time in pain.

(*The Washington Post*, December 18, 1994)

Prayer

The need for a moral revival is a major factor in my commitment to voluntary prayer in school.

(*Mother Jones*, November 1984)

Most people don't realize it's illegal to pray [in school].

((Excerpt from NBC's *Meet the Press*/Quoted on CNBC's *Rivera Live*, December 6, 1994)

☆ ☆ ☆ ☆ ☆ ☆ ☆ ☆ ☆ ☆

The Press

I start with the assumption that all human beings sin and that all human beings are, in fact, human. I assume that all reporters fit the same category.

(*The Washington Post*, Decembe 19, 1994)

You have to give the press confrontations. When you give them confrontations, you get attention; when you get attention, you can educate.

(NBC's *Meet the Press*, October 2, 1994)

I have to say as a Republican and a conservative, I think the press has, overall, been very tough on the President and on Mrs. Clinton.

(NBC's *Meet the Press*, December 4,. 1994)

It is much easier to communicate, in the current generation of news media, about scandal than about substance.

(*The New York Times*, August 23, 1992)

The number one fact about the news media is they love fights.

(*Mother Jones*, November 1984)

[This is] an age of extraordinarily cynical, adversarial press, an age of a White House press corps that devoured Carter, tried to devour Reagan and lost, devoured Bush and are now working on devouring Clinton.

(*The New York Times*, December 30, 1994)

Ronald Reagan

I love Ronald Reagan. I think Ronald Reagan is a great man who changed America.

(NBC's *Meet the Press*, December 1, 1991)

☆ ☆ ☆ ☆ ☆ ☆ ☆ ☆ ☆ ☆

Republicans

One of the great problems in the
Republican Party is that we don't
encourage you to be nasty.
    (Speech made to college Republicans/June 1978)

I was the middle linebacker of the
Republican Party. Now I'm head coach.
                (ABC's *Nightline*, November 29, 1994)

I am a Republican, but I think the greatest
failure of the last twenty years has been
the Republican Party, not the Democratic
Party. The Democratic Party has
attempted to do what the governing party
should do—govern. But it failed. And
when it failed, there was nobody there to
take up the burden. And I think that in
order for this civilization to survive, at
least as a free society, we've got to have a
more rigorous and cohesive sense of an
alternative party.
                        (*Changing of the Guard*, 1980)

☆　☆　☆　☆　☆　☆　☆　☆　☆　☆

We'll either be the strongest Republican
minority since 1954 or we're going to be
the majority. Our working assumption is
that we'll be a majority.

(*The New York Times*, October 27, 1994)

The great Republican tradition which my
family identified with in Pennsylvania was
the 1856-to-1912 tradition that was very
progressive. It was the party of
industrialization, of economic growth. It
was the party of the full lunch pail. And
that party was very activist. That was the
party that created the land-grant colleges
and built the transcontinental railroad. It
had a vision which it was willing to
impose upon the society.

(*Changing of the Guard*, 1980)

For the last fifty years the Republican
Party has been hypnotized by Franklin
Roosevelt, and its entire vision has been to
stop what he began.

(*Changing of the Guard*, 1980)

☆ ☆ ☆ ☆ ☆ ☆ ☆ ☆ ☆ ☆

We'll try to make sure the country
understands what the option is—the
option being do you want to continue
down a road of chaos and confusion, or do
you want to have policies that are closer to
what you believe in?
(Commenting on the November 1994 election/ABC's
This Week with David Brinkley, August 14, 1994)

We don't tell the truth hard enough, often
enough or aggressive enough about
Congress ... we don't recruit deeply
enough. I mean, we're up against Franklin
Roosevelt's legacy: big-city machines,
unions, incumbents ...
(Commenting on why the Republicans are not the
congressional majority/NBC's *Meet the Press*,
December 1, 1991)

Revolution

Real revolutions are made by the young.
They are made by the energetic. They are
made by the risk-takers.
(*The New York Times*, August 23, 1992)

☆ ☆ ☆ ☆ ☆ ☆ ☆ ☆ ☆ ☆ ☆

Franklin D. Roosevelt

You can never study Franklin Delano
Roosevelt too much. He did bring us out
of the Depression. He did lead the Allied
movement in World War II. In many ways
he created the modern world. He was
clearly, I think, as a political leader the
greatest figure of the twentieth century.

(*The New York Times*, December 6, 1994)

Scandal

Don't focus in only on scandal on the Hill.
They are interesting. They're great soap
opera. They're important, but they have to
be attached to people's lives.

(Congressional candidates' training session,
April 1992)

☆ ☆ ☆ ☆ ☆ ☆ ☆ ☆ ☆ ☆

Social Security

I think eventually you can reexamine
Social Security, in six to eight years. But I
think that the current generation of
politicians does not have the moral
standing, doesn't have the trust, to open
up the largest trust fund and the largest
social insurance program in the country.
And I think if you'd try to do it, you'd just
get into a brutal, nasty, mean fight, and
you'd lose.

(Interview on C-SPAN, the public affairs cable television system, January 1, 1995)

Soviet Union

The most dangerous summit for the West
since Adolf Hitler met with [British Prime
Minister Neville] Chamberlain in 1938 at
Munich.

(Commenting on the Gorbachev/Reagan
Summit/Quoted in the 1989 *Current
Biography Yearbook*)

☆ ☆ ☆ ☆ ☆ ☆ ☆ ☆ ☆ ☆

Space

If we will make an intensive effort to develop space we will create millions of jobs on earth while creating thousands of jobs in space, while at the same time ensuring a solid balance of payments in foreign trade by producing goods and services others want but cannot produce for themselves.

> (*Window of Opportunity: A Blueprint for the Future*, by Newt Gingrich, Tor/A Tom Doherty Associates Book/Published in Association with Baen Enterprises, 1984)

Speaker of the House

I want to be speaker. That's where the power is.

(Responding to Lee Howell, Gingrich's former press secretary, on why he doesn't want to be President, 1974/As discussed on *Dateline NBC*, November 15, 1994)

It's the American people's revolution.

> (On his election to Speaker of the House, *CBS This Morning*, November 9, 1994)

★　★　★　★　★　★　★　★　★　★

You have an obligation to the country. I mean, the Speaker of the House, because you're second in line after the vice president ... I have an institutional obligation to cooperate with the President of the United States on the foreign policy, the defense policy, the intelligence policies of the United States in a way that you have to bear a very different burden than if you are simply the partisan leader in opposition. ... it's more than I thought it would be. It's a bigger responsibility and a bigger job. You have an obligation, I think, not to give up on any of your ideology. We should cooperate, but not compromise.

(ABC's *Nightline*, November 29, 1994)

Because I am now the next Speaker, I am learning that everything I say has to be worded carefully and thought through at a level that I've never experienced in my life.

(ABC's *Nightline*, November 29, 1994)

It seems to me you've got to try to do it,
but you'd better be a little sobered and a
little humble about the size of it and listen
to a lot of advice, which is what I'm trying
to do.

(ABC's *Nightline*, November 29, 1994)

☆ ☆ ☆ ☆ ☆ ☆ ☆ ☆ ☆ ☆

Special Prosecutors

We either ought to abolish special prosecutor laws for everybody or we ought to apply them to the Congress. And I think you can make a case that the special prosecutor law has been bad, I think it has been, but if we're going to keep it, then by God, it ought to apply to the United States Congress. It ought to apply to members who almost certainly have an IRS problem, have a federal disclosure problem and, in some cases again, I'm told, both by news sources and by some people on the Ethics Committee, there are some indications that some members were borrowing money in September and October by putting in checks that were bad and then were giving that money to their campaign, loaning to their campaign, winning reelection and then repaying the money back to the bank as an interest-free election loan.

(ABC's *This Week with David Brinkley*, March 15, 1992)

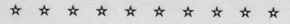

Taxes

I don't think $20,000 is exactly taxing the rich ... the country, if it's mad about taxes, should vote Republican.
(ABC's *This Week with David Brinkley*,
October 21, 1990)

What this country desperately needs is to have tax changes that change behavior, that increase building factories, increase creating jobs, increase people having take-home pay that encourages work.
(ABC's *This Week with David Brinkley*,
December 22, 1991)

Television

Practice whatever the big truth is so that you can say it in forty seconds on camera.
(Advice to Republican congressmen, 1989)

C-Span is more real than being there.
(Quoted in the *Atlanta Journal and Constitution*,
1985, as reported in *The Washington Post*,
December 20, 1994)

☆ ☆ ☆ ☆ ☆ ☆ ☆ ☆ ☆ ☆

The minute Tip O'Neill attacked me, he
and I got ninety seconds at the close of all
three network news shows.

(Commenting on former Speaker of the House
O'Neill's criticism that Gingrich appeared,
in front of a television camera, to be attacking a
silent group of Democrats, when in fact the chamber
was empty. Made to a group of conservative
activists, as reported by David Osborne in
Mother Jones, November 1984)

The great Rooseveltian majority was build
on that generation's equivalent of thirty-
second spots.

(NBC's *Meet the Press*, June 17, 1990)

I don't know how many million dollars in
advertising NBC has taken from various
companies, but I'd ask you: Given all that
money, which pays your salary, can you be
objective? I think you'd say sure, you can.
I find this very bizarre double standard
where people whose newspapers and
whose television stations take advertising
from virtually anybody and are somehow
pristine, pure, but then they turn to
politics.

(NBC's *Meet the Press*, June 19, 1994)

85

Term Limitations

I'm prepared to say that if Newt Gingrich's career existed under term limits, I would be very comfortable and very happy with that, and I'm prepared to say that I think it's a good system. The notion that everybody who's for something has to offer to commit suicide in order for you to think they're sincere, I think, is fairly outrageous. The fact is, I'm prepared to suggest very large changes. I've seen the system for a long time. I think it'll survive with term limits. It does in the White House. We have eight-year limits on the presidency. That doesn't seem to stop us. And both Eisenhower and Reagan might well have won a third term. But I don't think anybody seriously believes that we ought to, in fact, repeal the eight-year limit on Presidents.

(NBC's *Meet the Press*, October 2, 1994)

★   ★   ★   ★   ★   ★   ★   ★   ★   ★

United Nations

The United Nations is a totally
incompetent instrument anyplace that
matters. When you get a serious problem
with serious violence, the United Nations
is literally incompetent, and it kills people
by its behavior.

(NBC's *Meet the Press*, December 4, 1994)

USSR

We must expect the Soviet system to
survive in its present brutish form for a
very long time. There will be Soviet labor
camps and Soviet torture chambers well
into our great-grandchildren's lives.

(*The Washington Post*, December 20, 1994)

War

You grow up an army brat named Newton
and you learn about combat.

(Quoted in *Newsweek*, January 9, 1995)

I left that battlefield convinced that men do horrible things to each other, that great nations can spend their lifeblood and their treasure on efforts to coerce and subjugate their fellow man.

(Commenting on a visit to the World War I battlefield at Verdun, which prompted his decision to enter politics/*Mother Jones*, November 1984)

We made a mistake going into Lebanon. I think we could make a mistake going into the Balkans. We should just be very sure before we start that we know where it's going to get us and that we're prepared to do what it takes to be successful.

(CBS's *Face the Nation*, May 9, 1993)

☆ ☆ ☆ ☆ ☆ ☆ ☆ ☆ ☆ ☆

Washington

In this cold and ruthless city, the center of hypocrisy is Capitol Hill.

> (PBS's *Ethics in America*, February 1989)

In this city, if you are the conservative spokesman, you're going to get your brains blown out.

> (Speaking of John Sununu/NBC's *Meet the Press*, Decmeber 1, 1991)

I'm not up here to do anything that's essentially personalistic, or that's built around short-run Band-Aids. My friends and I are trying to figure out strategically what we have to do in this country in the next ten years to build a majority.

> (*Changing of the Guard*, 1980)

A large, open conspiracy to take away the money and freedom of the citizens of this country.

> (Quoted in the 1989 *Current Biography Yearbook*)

Washington, frankly, is a city that could do
with fresh blood and fresh ideas.
> (NPR's *All Things Considered*,
> with Robert Siegel, October 11, 1990)

I think that the system in Washington is,
frankly, so out of touch with America and
so pathetically sick that the country
genuinely believes you've got to break up
the current generation of professional
politicians.
> (NBC's *Meet the Press*, October 2, 1994)

The Welfare State

It's only in the welfare state that we
reduce things to their dumbest
denominators.
> (NBC's *Meet the Press*, February 21, 1993)

☆ ☆ ☆ ☆ ☆ ☆ ☆ ☆ ☆ ☆

My father, who is here today, was a foster child who was adopted as a teenager. I am adopted. We have relatives who are adopted. We are not talking out of some vague, impersonal, Dickens *Bleak House*, middle-class, intellectual model. We have lived the alternatives.

(Excerpt from Gingrich's opening day speech to the 104th Congress/*The New York Times*, January 5, 1995)

Detroit's great problems, the collapse of the welfare state, the level of violent crime, the amount of drugs, the problems of bureaucracy, the high taxes—those problems aren't made in Japan, they're made in Detroit, they're made in America. We've got to replace the welfare state if we're ever going to be competitive in the world market.

(ABC's *Nightline*, January 6, 1992)

★　★　★　★　★　★　★　★　★　★

I think there's a broad consensus in this
country to stop the inflow of illegal aliens
and to stop subsidizing illegal aliens by
paying them, putting them on welfare.

(ABC's *This Week with David Brinkley*,
January 2, 1994)

I'm less worried about cutting off women
than I am about sending the signal to
twelve-, thirteen-, fourteen-, and fifteen-
year olds that this is not desirable, this is
not going to be subsidized, this is not
something that you should engage in in
fifth, sixth, and seventh grades.

(ABC's *This Week with David Brinkley*,
January 2, 1994)

We will not make it through your lifetime
without radical change. You're either
going to force the changes, or your
generation is going to suffer a long, steady
decline in the quality of life.

(Comments to the Capitol Hill Club, 1992)

In terms of real money the welfare budget is AFDC, WIC, Medicaid, public housing—there's a whole range of things, it's not just one item. And this again is like the welfare state, you don't see it; it's a shell game and the taxpayer never quite gets to see the pea.

(NBC's *Meet the Press*, February 21, 1993)

I don't think the American people, when they talk about welfare reform, want to see us create a new welfare health system designed by the Clintons with a hundred million people getting a brand-new entitlement.

(NBC's *Meet the Press*, June 19, 1994)

★ ★ ★ ★ ★ ★ ★ ★ ★ ★

Jim Wright

People warned me off from this. They said
I'd be asking for political trouble. But I
didn't come here to pleasantly rise on an
escalator of self-serving compromises.

> (Commenting on his campaign to remove Jim
> Wright to Peter Osterlund of *The Christian Science
> Monitor*, May 31, 1989)

When I talked about Democrats who have
significant ethics problems, in case after
case, they've either turned our to be
convicted felons, people who had to
resign, people who had Ethics Committee
reports against them, people who were
censored or, in the case of Speaker
Wright, somebody who has literally had to
resign under pressure because of what he
had done, broke the rules. It wasn't a
question of appearance. He broke the
rules.

> (NBC's *Meet the Press*, October 2, 1994)

I've got a lot in my background that isn't pleasant. But there's nothing like the genuine corruption of Jim Wright.

(*The Washington Post*, December 20, 1994)